STATE OFFICERS.

Governor .... GEORGE H. HODGES.... Olathe.
Lieutenant Governor .... SHEFFIELD INGALLS... Atchison.
Secretary of State.......... CHAS. H. SESSIONS... Topeka.
State Auditor .... W. E. DAVIS......... Dodge City.
State Treasurer .... EARL AKERS .... Stafford.
Attorney-general .... JOHN S. DAWSON..... Hill City.
Supt. of Public Instruction.. W. D. ROSS.......... Topeka.
Supt. of Insurance.......... IKE S. LEWIS........ St. John.
State Printer .... W. C. AUSTIN........ Cottonwood Falls.

BOARDS COMPOSED OF STATE OFFICERS.

EXECUTIVE COUNCIL—The Governor, Secretary of State, State Auditor, State Treasurer, Attorney-general, and Superintendent of Public Instruction.

SCHOOL FUND COMMISSIONERS—Secretary of State, Attorney-general, and Superintendent of Public Instruction.

STATE CHARTER BOARD—Attorney-general, Secretary of State, and Bank Commissioner.

SINKING FUND COMMISSIONERS—Governor, Secretary of State, and State Auditor.

STATE BOARD OF TREASURY EXAMINERS—Governor, Secretary of State, and State Auditor.

STATE PRINTING COMMISSION—State Printer, Secretary of State, and Attorney-general.

STATE LAND OFFICE—State Auditor, *ex officio* Register.

STATE BLANK BOOK COMMISSION—State Accountant, State Printer, and Attorney-general.

STATE BOARD OF CANVASSERS—Governor, Secretary of State, State Auditor, State Treasurer, and Attorney-general.

STATE MOVING PICTURE CENSORSHIP COMMISSION—Governor, Secretary of State, and Attorney-general.

STATE PRINTING COMMISSION FOR UNIFORM COUNTY RECORDS—Attorney-general, State Printer, and State Accountant.

4

OFFICERS APPOINTED BY THE GOVERNOR.

BANK COMMISSIONER—Chas. M. Sawyer, Norton.

COMMISSIONER OF LABOR AND INDUSTRY—W. L. O'Brien, Topeka.

STATE MINE INSPECTOR—Francis M. Keegan, Pittsburg.

LIVE STOCK SANITARY COMMISSIONER—Sam S. Graybill, Hutchinson.

INSPECTOR OF OILS—Frank Cumiskey, Pittsburg.

ADJUTANT GENERAL—C. I. Martin, Fort Scott.

STATE ACCOUNTANT—Jasper T. Kincaid, Olathe.

STATE ARCHITECT—Charles H. Chandler, Topeka.

HOTEL COMMISSIONER—Miles H. Mulroy, Hays.

STATE FIRE MARSHAL—Harrison Parkman, Emporia.

STATE AGENT AT WASHINGTON—John C. Nicholson, Newton.

BOARD OF EDUCATIONAL ADMINISTRATION.

(Appointed by Governor.)

ED. T. HACKNEY, *Chairman*...................... Wellington.
CORA G. LEWIS................................... Kinsley.
E. W. HOCH..................................... Marion.
D. M. BOWEN, *Secretary* (appointed by board)....... Pittsburg.

INSTITUTIONS UNDER BOARD OF EDUCATIONAL ADMINISTRATION.

UNIVERSITY OF KANSAS—Frank Strong, Chancellor, Lawrence.

KANSAS STATE AGRICULTURAL COLLEGE—H. J. Waters, President, Manhattan.

STATE NORMAL SCHOOL—T. W. Butcher, President, Emporia.

PITTSBURG MANUAL TRAINING NORMAL SCHOOL—W. A. Brandenburg, President.

WESTERN NORMAL SCHOOL, Hays—W. A. Lewis, Principal.

SCHOOL FOR DEAF, Olathe—Mrs. Kate S. Herman, Superintendent.

SCHOOL FOR BLIND, Kansas City—Mrs. Grace Norton Roseberry, Superintendent.

KANSAS MEDICAL SCHOOL, Rosedale—S. J. Crumbine, Dean.

SCHOOL OF MINES, Weir—Burton Lee Wolfe, Principal.

STATE FISH HATCHERY, Pratt—L. L. Dyche, Fish and Game Warden.

IRRIGATION EXPERIMENT STATION, Tribune—C. E. Cassel, Superintendent.

IRRIGATION EXPERIMENT STATION, Garden City—E. T. Chilcott, Superintendent.

FORESTRY EXPERIMENT STATION, Dodge City—F. J. Turner, Forester.

AGRICULTURAL EXPERIMENT STATION, Colby. ———

AGRICULTURAL EXPERIMENT STATION, Lakin. ———
AGRICULTURAL EXPERIMENT STATION, Fort Hays—Geo. K. Helder, Superintendent.
STATE DAIRY COMMISSIONER—George S. Hine, Manhattan.
STATE GEOLOGIST—Eramus Haworth, Lawrence.
STATE ENTOMOLOGIST—S. J. Hunter, Lawrence.
STATE VETERINARIAN—F. S. Schoenlieber, Manhattan.
STATE HIGHWAY ENGINEER, W. S. Gearhart, Manhattan.

BOARD OF TRUSTEES INDUSTRIAL DEPARTMENT WESTERN UNIVERSITY.
(Appointed by Governor.)

FRED K. DOUGLAS.............................. Kansas City.
A. D. GRIFFIN................................. Topeka.
CLEMENT WILLIAMS .... Kansas City.
J. G. GROVES .... Edwardsville.

INSTITUTION UNDER BOARD.
QUINDARO COLORED UNIVERSITY—H. T. Kealing, President.

BOARD OF TRUSTEES INDUSTRIAL AND EDUCATIONAL INSTITUTE, TOPEKA.
(Appointed by Governor.)

J. B. LARIMER................................. Topeka.
JOHN M. WRIGHT............................... Topeka.
J. V. ABRAHAMS............................... Topeka.
CLYDE W. MILLER.............................. Topeka.

INSTITUTION UNDER BOARD.
TOPEKA COLORED INDUSTRIAL SCHOOL—W. R. Carter, Superintendent.

STATE BOARD OF EDUCATION.
State Superintendent, W. D. ROSS, *President, ex officio,* Topeka.
Chancellor, FRANK STRONG, *ex officio*............... Lawrence.
President, T. W. BUTCHER, *ex officio*................ Emporia.
President, H. J. WATERS, *ex officio*................ Manhattan.
(Appointed by Governor.)
JOHN MACDONALD .... Topeka.
MRS. GRACE SNYDER........................... Cawker City.
MISS EFFIE MAHAFFIE......................... Kansas City.

STATE SCHOOL BOOK COMMISSION.

W. D. Ross, *ex officio*............................. Topeka.
H. J. Waters, *ex officio*........................... Manhattan.
T. W. Butcher, *ex officio*......................... Emporia.
W. C. Austin, *ex officio*........................... Cottonwood Falls.
Geo. B. Ross, *ex officio*........................... Sterling.
(Appointed by Governor.)
Cora Wellhouse Bullard...................... Tonganoxie.
C. A. Cain... Topeka.
A. M. Thoroman, *Secretary* (appointed by commission), Cottonwood Falls.

BOARD OF CONTROL.
(Appointed by Governor.)

W. E. Brooks, *Chairman*......................... Fort Scott.
Stance Meyers .... Leavenworth.
H. C. Bowman................................... Newton.
J. W. Howe, *Secretary* (appointed by board)........ Abilene.

INSTITUTIONS UNDER THE BOARD OF CONTROL.

Topeka State Hospital, Topeka, T. C. Biddle, Superintendent, Topeka.

Osawatomie State Hospital, Osawatomie, T. A. Carmichael, Superintendent, Goodland.

Parsons State Hospital (sane and insane epileptic), Parsons, Dr. M. L. Perry, Superintendent, Parsons.

School for Feeble-minded Youth, Winfield, Dr. Fred Cave, Superintendent, Winfield, Kan.

Soldiers' Orphans' Home, Atchison, Mrs. E. K. Burns, Atchison.

Larned State Hospital, Larned, B. F. Hawk, Superintendent, Kingman.

State Tubercular Sanitarium, Norton, C. S. Kenney, Superintendent, Norton.

STATE BOARD OF CORRECTIONS.
(Appointed by Governor.)

W. L. Brown, *Chairman*......................... Kingman.
J. E. Porter..................................... Kansas City.
Chas. M. Harger................................. Abilene.

INSTITUTIONS UNDER BOARD OF CORRECTIONS.

Penitentiary, Lansing, J. D. Botkin, Warden.
Reformatory, Hutchinson, J. N. Herr, Superintendent.
Industrial School for Boys, Topeka, H. W. Charles, Superintendent.
Industrial School for Girls, Beloit, Miss Frank Wilson, Superintendent.

MANAGERS STATE SOLDIERS' HOME AND MOTHER BICKERDYKE HOME.
(Appointed by Governor.)

W. E. BROOKS, *Chairman*.......................... Fort Scott.
STANCE MEYERS .... Leavenworth.
D. M. BENDER................................... Parsons.

INSTITUTIONS UNDER BOARD OF MANAGERS.
STATE SOLDIERS' HOME, Fort Dodge, Ansel F. Hatton, Commandant, Fort Dodge.
MOTHER BICKERDYKE HOME, Ellsworth, J. C. Chase, Superintendent, Ellsworth.

PUBLIC UTILITIES COMMISSION.
(Appointed by Governor.)

HENDERSON S. MARTIN............................ Marion.
JOHN M. KINKEL................................. Hutchinson.
JAMES A. CABLE................................. Kansas City.
W. P. FEDER, *Secretary* (appointed by commission)... Great Bend.

TAX COMMISSION.
(Appointed by Governor.)

SAMUEL T. HOWE................................. Topeka.
J. A. BURNETTE................................. Caldwell.
J. H. HOSTETLER................................ Belleville.
CLARENCE SMITH, *Secretary* (appointed by commission), Topeka.

IRRIGATION BOARD.
(Appointed by Governor.)

F. A. HINES, *Chairman*......................... Scott City.
BURT P. WALKER, *Secretary*..................... Osborne.
J. B. HAMMOND.................................. Syracuse.

STATE GRAIN GRADING COMMISSION.
(Appointed by Governor.)

J. B. NICHOLSON................................ Topeka.
A. T. ROGERS................................... Beloit.
A. C. BAILEY................................... Kinsley.

8

BOARD OF BARBER EXAMINERS.
(Appointed by Governor.)

C. C. Moyer...................................... Wichita.
C. H. Mathews.................................... Topeka.
F. W. Koester.................................... Atchison.

PANAMA PACIFIC EXPOSITION COMMISSION.
(Appointed by Governor.)

Geo. H. Hodges, *ex officio, Chairman*................ Topeka.
Albert T. Reid................................... Topeka.
W. E. Benson..................................... El Dorado.
J. L. Pettyjohn.................................. Olathe.
Walter Innes..................................... Wichita.
H. E. Dean, *Secretary*........................... Kansas City.

STATE BOARD OF HEALTH.
(Appointed by Governor.)

B. J. Alexander, M. D., *President,*................ Hiawatha.
S. J. Crumbine, *Secretary* (elected by board)........ Topeka.
C. H. Lerrigo, M. D.............................. Topeka.
Clay E. Coburn, M. D............................ Kansas City.
W. O. Thompson, M. D............................ Dodge City.
O. D. Walker, M. D.............................. Salina.
J. S. Cummings, M. D............................ Bronson.
Jesse Thomas Orr, M. D.......................... Olathe.
V. C. Eddy, M. D................................ Colby.
Walter D. Hunt, M. D........................... Emporia.
C. D. Welch, *Attorney*......................... Coffeyville.

ADVISORY COMMISSION OF THE KANSAS SANATORIUM FOR TUBERCULOSIS PATIENTS.
(Appointed by Governor.)

Dr. W. H. Bauer................................ Sylvia.
Dr. John Sippy................................. Belle Plaine.
Dr. D. M. Hart................................. Macksville.
Dr. J. A. Milligan............................. Garnett.

BOARD OF MEDICAL EXAMINATION AND REGISTRATION.

(Appointed by Governor.)

Dr. H. A. Dykes, Regular, *Secretary*............... Lebanon.
Dr. A. J. Anderson, Regular..................... Lawrence.
Dr. A. S. Ross, Eclectic......................... Sabetha.
Dr. L. A. Ryder, Homeopathy..................... Topeka.
Dr. L. P. Gaillardet, Regular................... Plainville.
Dr. E. P. Hatfield, Eclectic..................... Olathe.
Dr. Joseph E. Sawtell......................... Kansas City.

BOARD OF PHARMACY.

(Appointed by Governor.)

W. E. Sherriff, *Secretary*....................... Ellsworth.
Max W. Friedenburg........................... Winfield.
W. S. Henrion................................. Wichita.
W. S. Dick................................... Lawrence.
Geo. H. Bunch................................. Beloit.

BOARD OF OSTEOPATHIC EXAMINATION AND REGISTRATION.

(Appointed by Governor.)

F. M. Godfrey................................. Holton.
E. B. Waters................................. Wichita.
J. L. McClanahan .... Paola.
Miss Linda Hardy............................. Hiawatha.
C. E. Hulett................................. Topeka.

BOARD OF CHIROPRACTIC EXAMINERS.

(No appointments made by Governor.)

BOARD OF OPTOMETRY.

(Appointed by Governor.)

Thomas Gowenlock .... Clay Center.
F. W. Hunt................................... Burlingame.
J. S. Johnson................................. Leroy.

BOARD OF DENTISTRY.

(Appointed by Governor.)

Dr. G. F. Ambrose............................ El Dorado.
Dr. F. O. Hetrick............................ Ottawa.
Dr. J. Fremont Burket......................... Kingman.

BOARD OF EXAMINERS, TRAINED NURSES.
(Appointed by Governor.)

Mrs. Kate Williams............................. Hutchinson.
Miss E. Eason................................., ... Kansas City.
Miss M. M. Conklin............................. Topeka.
Mrs. A. R. O'Keefe, *Secretary*.................... Wichita.

STATE BOARD OF EMBALMING.
(Appointed by Governor.)

Joe S. Johnson..................................... Osawatomie.
Geo. W. Southern.............................. Manhattan.
T. B. Oldroyd.................................. Arkansas City.

STATE VETERINARY BOARD.
(Appointed by Governor.)

B. A. Robinson.................................. Independence.
O. O. Wolf, *Secretary*........................... Ottawa.
Arthur A. Shetler............................... Wellington.

STATE BOARD OF AGRICULTURE.
(Officers elected by Board.)

Geo. B. Ross, *President*.......................... Sterling.
A. W. Smith, *Vice President*..................... McPherson.
J. T. Tredway, *Treasurer*........................ La Harpe.
F. D. Coburn, *Secretary*......................... Topeka.

HORTICULTURAL SOCIETY.
(Officers elected by Society.)

J. T. Tredway, *President*........................ La Harpe.
G. J. Smith, *Vice President*..................... Lawrence.
Edwin Snyder, *Treasurer*........................ Topeka.
Walter Wellhouse, *Secretary*.................... Topeka.

MEMORIAL HALL BUILDING COMMISSION.
(Membership fixed by law.)

Governor Geo. H. Hodges, *President*................ Olathe.
Lieut. Governor Sheffield Ingalls................ Atchison.
Speaker of the House, W. L. Brown................ Kingman.
State Senator, Paul Klein........................ Iola.
Member of the House, F. H. Chase................. Hoyt.
Dept. Com. Grand Army Republic, J. N. Harrison.... Topeka.

LEGISLATIVE DIRECTORY.

SENATE, 1913-1915.

Dist.	Name.	Post office.
1.	W. P. Lambertson	Fairview.
2.	B. P. Waggener	Atchison.
3.	Vinton Stillings	Leavenworth.
4.	T. A. Milton	Kansas City.
5.	Benjamin E. Wilson	Williamstown.
6.	M. J. Williams	Louisburg.
7.	Noah L. Bowman	Garnett.
8.	J. M. Davis	Bronson.
9.	E. F. Porter	Pittsburg.
10.	Chas. S. Huffman	Columbus.
11.	I. M. Hinds	Mound Valley.
12.	Jno. F. Overfield	Independence.
13.	Ben S. Paulen	Fredonia.
14.	Paul Klein	Iola.
15.	O. O. Wolf	Ottawa.
16.	J. H. Stavely	Lyndon.
17.	James A. Troutman	Topeka.
18.	James M. Meek	Centralia.
19.	R. S. Pauley	Beattie.
20.	Walter E. Wilson	Washington.
21.	Loring Trott	Junction City.
22.	J. W. Howe	Abilene.
23.	Arthur R. Kinkel	Council Grove.
24.	William M. Price	Madison.
25.	J. D. Joseph	White Water.
26.	John T. Denton	Grenola.
27.	L. P. King	Winfield.
28.	Geo. Nixon	Peck.
29.	Frank Nighswonger	Wichita.
30.	Lacey M. Simpson	Canton.
31.	Harry McMillan	Minneapolis.
32.	Albert B. Carney	Concordia.
33.	E. C. Logan	Solomon Rapids.
34.	Harry Gray	Luray.
35.	H. F. Sutton	St. John.
36.	Emerson Carey	Hutchinson.
37.	Francis C. Price	Ashland.
38.	Jouett Shouse	Kinsley.
39.	James Malone	Herndon.
40.	I. M. Mahin	Smith Center.

HOUSE OF REPRESENTATIVES, 1913.

Dist.	County.	Name.	Post office.
1.	Doniphan	S. M. Brewster	Troy.
2.	Atchison	James W. Orr	Atchison.
3.	Atchison	U. B. Sharpless	Atchison.
4.	Jefferson	Clarence S. Moyer	Nortonville.
5.	Leavenworth	Edward Carroll	Leavenworth.
6.	Leavenworth	J. M. Gilman	Leavenworth.
7.	Wyandotte	W. W. Gordon	Kansas City.
8.	Wyandotte	Charles S. Holbrook	Kansas City.
9.	Wyandotte	J. N. Atkinson	Kansas City.
10.	Johnson	Jasper T. Kincaid	Olathe.
11.	Douglas	J. R. Topping	Lawrence.
12.	Douglas	John M. Newlin	Lawrence.
13.	Franklin	W. G. Tulloss	Rantoul.
14.	Miami	Robert O'Connor	Edgerton.
15.	Linn	Robert J. Tyson	Goodrich.
16.	Anderson	E. M. Bentley	Welda.
17.	Allen	J. W. Hamm	Humboldt.
18.	Bourbon	A. M. Keene	Fort Scott.
19.	Bourbon	J. S. Cummings	Bronson.
20.	Crawford	B. F. Wilson	Girard.
21.	Crawford	J. Albert Gibson	Pittsburg.
22.	Cherokee	Everett Miller	Scammon.
23.	Cherokee	R. L. Armstrong	Faulkner.
24.	Labette	J. I. Tanner	Cherryvale.
25.	Labette	R. M. Noble	Bartlett.
26.	Montgomery	A. M. Ragle	Coffeyville.
27.	Montgomery	O. V. Stevens	Caney.
28.	Neosho	A. H. Turner	Chanute.
29.	Wilson	Walter J. Burtis	Fredonia.
30.	Woodson	G. H. Tannahill	Vernon.
31.	Coffey	J. A. Mahurin	Sharpe.
32.	Osage	F. H. Woodbury	Olivet.
33.	Shawnee	Fred Voiland	Topeka.
34.	Shawnee	C. G. Blakely	Topeka.
35.	Shawnee	Robert Stone	Topeka.
36.	Jackson	F. H. Chase	Hoyt.
37.	Brown	J. F. Bailey	Horton.
38.	Nemaha	R. W. Moorhead	Sabetha.
39.	Marshall	J. J. Tilley	Frankfort.
40.	Marshall	N. S. Kerschen	Marysville.
41.	Pottawatomie	Walter Robson	Westmoreland.
42.	Riley	V. E. Johnson	Randolph.
43.	Geary	Mike Frey	Junction City.
44.	Wabaunsee	George G. Bunger	Eskridge.
45.	Lyon	D. W. Spiker	Emporia.
46.	Lyon	T. Jensen	Emporia.
47.	Greenwood	Robt. Focht	Eureka.

Dist.	County.	Name.	Post office.
48.	Elk	Lewis Kyser	Howard.
49.	Chautauqua	Wm. McDannald	Peru.
50.	Cowley	O. S. Gibson	Arkansas City.
51.	Cowley	Elisha Harned	Atlanta.
52.	Butler	W. J. Houston	Potwin.
53.	Butler	J. M. Satterthwaite	Douglas.
54.	Chase	J. B. Hanna	Cedar Point.
55.	Marion	Taylor Riddle	Marion.
56.	Morris	W. H. Dodderidge	White City.
57.	Dickinson	L. P. Houtz	Abilene.
58.	Clay	J. W. Carnahan	Clay Center.
59.	Washington	M. O. Reitzel	Washington.
60.	Republic	H. N. Boyd	Belleville.
61.	Cloud	C. F. Armstrong	Clyde.
62.	Ottawa	C. N. Miller	Minneapolis.
63.	Saline	W. H. Todd	Salina.
64.	McPherson	John Ostlind, Jr.	McPherson.
65.	Harvey	N. G. Perryman	Newton.
66.	Sedgwick	I. N. Williams	Wichita.
67.	Sedgwick	S. T. Jocelyn	Wichita.
68.	Sedgwick	Theodore Ossweiler	Garden Plain.
69.	Sumner	Chas. Hangen	Wellington.
70.	Sumner	Robt. McGregor	South Haven.
71.	Harper	T. W. Bay	Corwin.
72.	Kingman	W. L. Brown	Kingman.
73.	Barber	J. N. Herr	Kiowa.
74.	Pratt	Wm. Barrett	Pratt.
75.	Reno	J. P. O. Graber	Hutchinson.
76.	Reno	G. E. Blaisdell	Sylvia.
77.	Stafford	R. L. Milton	Stafford.
78.	Barton	Fred Zutavern	Great Bend.
79.	Rice	George B. Ross	Sterling.
80.	Ellsworth	R. J. Smischny	Wilson.
81.	Russell	Henry M. Laing	Russell.
82.	Lincoln	W. E. Lyon	Lincoln.
83.	Mitchell	John Tromble	Asherville.
84.	Osborne	F. A. Dawley	Waldo.
85.	Jewell	W. R. Mitchell	Mankato.
86.	Smith	Frank E. Lumpkin	Bellaire.
87.	Phillips	Frank Strain	Phillipsburg.
88.	Rooks	H. T. Sutor	Palco.
89.	Ellis	Miles H. Mulroy	Hays.
90.	Rush	J. H. Timken	Bison.
91.	Pawnee	A. A. Doerr	Larned.
92.	Edwards	N. A. Davis	Kinsley.
93.	Kiowa	Henry W. Wacker	Greensburg.
94.	Comanche	Geo. H. Helton	Coldwater.
95.	Clark	F. E. Dailey	Lexington.
96.	Ford	T. S. Lane	Bucklin.

Dist.	County.	Name.	Post office.
97.	Hodgeman	A. B. Scott	Jetmore.
98.	Ness	C. D. Foster	Ness City.
99.	Trego	O. L. Cook	Wa Keeney.
100.	Graham	John R. Ashcroft	Hill City.
101.	Norton	W. R. Dowling	Norcatur.
102.	Decatur	J. M. Shuey	Norcatur.
103.	Sheridan	J. W. Schlicher	Hoxie.
104.	Gove	George P. Crippen	Quinter.
105.	Thomas	A. Showalter	Colby.
106.	Rawlins	Robert S. Hendricks	Atwood.
107.	Cheyenne	J. E. Uplinger	St. Francis.
108.	Sherman	Wm. H. Stone	Goodland.
109.	Logan	W. E. Fallas	Oakley.
110.	Wallace	Thos. L. Carney	Wallace.
111.	Wichita	C. A. Freeland	Leoti.
112.	Greeley	Clement L. Wilson	Tribune.
113.	Scott	F. A. Hines	Scott City.
114.	Lane	O. P. Jewett	Dighton.
115.	Finney	J. C. Tyler	Garden City.
116.	Kearny	T. N. Thorpe	Lakin.
117.	Hamilton	H. J. Lauback	Coolidge.
118.	Grant	P. A. Walker	New Ulysses.
119.	Stanton	C. A. Gillum	Fisher.
120.	Gray	T. J. Davis	Cave.
121.	Haskell	S. A. McCollum	Santa Fe.
122.	Meade	E. L. Watts	Fowler.
123.	Seward	R. T. Nichols	Liberal.
124.	Stevens	J. W. Phillips	Hugoton.
125.	Morton	C. H. Drew	Richfield.

KANSAS FEDERAL OFFICERS.

UNITED STATES SENATORS.

Term expires.
JOSEPH L. BRISTOW, Salina........................... March 4, 1915.
WILLIAM H. THOMPSON, Garden City................... March 4, 1919.

REPRESENTATIVES IN CONGRESS.

Term expires.
D. R. ANTHONY, Jr., Leavenworth, first district........ March 4, 1915.
JOSEPH TAGGART, Kansas City, second district.......... March 4, 1915.
PHILIP P. CAMPBELL, Pittsburg, third district.......... March 4, 1915.
DUDLEY DOOLITTLE, Strong City, fourth district........ March 4, 1915.
G. T. HELVERING, Marysville, fifth district............. March 4, 1915.
JOHN R. CONNELLY, Colby, sixth district.............. March 4, 1915.
GEO. A. NEELEY, Hutchinson, seventh district.......... March 4, 1915.
VICTOR MURDOCK, Wichita, eighth district............. March 4, 1915.

UNITED STATES OFFICIALS IN KANSAS.
(Aside from the judiciary.)
Internal Revenue Collector............. W. H. L. Pepperell, Concordia.

LAND OFFICES.—Kansas is divided into two United States land-office districts:
The Dodge City land district comprises all of that territory in Kansas lying west of a line drawn from the northeast corner of Barton county due south to the Oklahoma state line, and from the northeast corner of Barton county due west to the Colorado line.

Register .... Henry F. Millikan, Dodge City.
Receiver .... L. J. Pettyjohn, Dodge City.

The Topeka district comprises all territory in the state of Kansas outside of the Dodge City district.

Register .... Geo. W. Fisher, Topeka.
Receiver .... J. G. Wood, Topeka.

UNITED STATES COURTS—KANSAS DISTRICT.

Office.   *Name.*   *Residence.*
Judge United States District Court, John C. Pollock...... Winfield.
District Attorney .... Fred Robertson ..... Atwood.
United States Marshal........... J. R. Harrison....... Topeka.
Clerk United States District Court, Morton Albaugh ..... Kingman.

TERMS OF UNITED STATES DISTRICT COURT.—The United States district court is held at Topeka on the second Monday of April; at Salina (by consent or special order), on the second Monday of May; at Wichita, on the second Monday of March and September; at Leavenworth, on the second Monday of October; and at Fort Scott, on the first Monday of May and second Monday of November.

(16)

THE KANSAS JUDICIARY.

THE SUPREME COURT.

Name.	Office.	Residence.
WILLIAM A. JOHNSTON	Chief Justice	Minneapolis.
ROUSSEAU A. BURCH	Justice	Salina.
HENRY F. MASON	"	Garden City.
CLARK A. SMITH	"	Cawker City.
SILAS PORTER	"	Kansas City.
ALFRED W. BENSON	"	Ottawa.
J. S. WEST	"	Topeka.
D. A. VALENTINE	Clerk of the Court	Clay Center.
OSCAR L. MOORE	Court Reporter	Abilene.

TERMS OF THE KANSAS SUPREME COURT.—First Tuesday of January and July, but court meets for hearing of cases in every month (August and September excepted), beginning on the first Monday of the month.

APPOINTED BY THE SUPREME COURT.

STATE LIBRARY.—Librarian, James L. King, Topeka.

LEGISLATIVE REFERENCE LIBRARY.—Cataloguer, Edwina M. Casey, Topeka.

TRAVELING LIBRARIES COMMISSION.—Secretary, Mrs. Adrian L. Greene, Topeka.

BOARD OF LAW EXAMINERS.—Jas. D. McFarland, chairman, Topeka; Wm. Easton Hutchison, Garden City; Geo. H. Buckman, Winfield; David M. Dale, Wichita; Austin M. Keene, Fort Scott.

KANSAS DISTRICT COURTS.

FIRST DISTRICT.

J. H. WENDORFF, Judge; residence, Leavenworth.

LEAVENWORTH COUNTY.—First Monday of January and second Monday of April and October.

SECOND DISTRICT.

W. A. JACKSON, Judge; residence, Atchison.

ATCHISON COUNTY.—Second Monday of January, April and September.

THIRD DISTRICT.

ALSTON W. DANA, Judge, first division; residence, Topeka.

GEORGE H. WHITCOMB, Judge, second division; residence, Topeka.

SHAWNEE COUNTY.—Second Monday of January, first Monday of April, and first Tuesday of September.

FOURTH DISTRICT.

CHARLES A. SMART, Judge; residence, Ottawa.

DOUGLAS COUNTY.—First Monday of February, May and November.

FRANKLIN COUNTY.—First Monday of January and April and second Monday of September.

ANDERSON COUNTY.—First Monday of March and second Monday of June and October.

FIFTH DISTRICT.

WILLIAM C. HARRIS, Judge; residence, Emporia.

COFFEY COUNTY.—First Tuesday of January, April and September.

LYON COUNTY.—First Tuesday of February, May and October.

CHASE COUNTY.—First Tuesday of March, June and November.

SIXTH DISTRICT.

C. E. HULETT, Judge; residence, Fort Scott.

BOURBON COUNTY.—First Monday of January, second Monday of May, and first Monday of October.

LINN COUNTY.—First Monday of April, second Monday of July, and first Monday of December.

SEVENTH DISTRICT.

J. W. FINLEY, Judge; residence, Chanute.

WILSON COUNTY.—First Tuesday of January, first Tuesday of April, and first Tuesday of September.

NEOSHO COUNTY.—Second Tuesday of February, second Tuesday of May, and second Tuesday of October.

EIGHTH DISTRICT.

R. L. KING, Judge; residence, Marion.

DICKINSON COUNTY.—First Monday of January, third Monday of May, and second Monday of September.

MARION COUNTY.—First Monday of February, May and October.

GEARY COUNTY.—First Monday of March and June and second Monday of November.

MORRIS COUNTY.—First Monday of April, third Monday of June, and first Monday of December.

NINTH DISTRICT.

F. F. PRIGG, Judge; residence, Hutchinson.

RENO COUNTY.—First Tuesday of January, April and September.

HARVEY COUNTY.—Second Tuesday of February and May and first Wednesday after the first Monday of November.

McPHERSON COUNTY.—Second Tuesday of March and first Tuesday of June and December.

TENTH DISTRICT.

J. O. RANKIN, Judge; residence, Paola.

JOHNSON COUNTY.—First Monday of January, May and September.

MIAMI COUNTY —First Monday of February and June and second Wednesday of November.

ELEVENTH DISTRICT.

E. E. SAPP, Judge; residence, Galena.

CHEROKEE COUNTY.—At Columbus, first Monday of January, May and October; at Galena, first Monday of March and September and second Wednesday of November.

TWELFTH DISTRICT.

JOHN C. HOGIN, Judge; residence, Belleville.

CLOUD COUNTY.—First Tuesday of January, April and September.

REPUBLIC COUNTY.—First Tuesday of February, May and October.

WASHINGTON COUNTY.—First Tuesday of March and June and the Tuesday succeeding the second Monday of November.

THIRTEENTH DISTRICT.

A. T. AYRES, Judge; residence, Howard.

CHAUTAUQUA COUNTY.—First Tuesday of February, third Tuesday of May, and first Tuesday of October.

ELK COUNTY.—Third Tuesday of January, first Tuesday of May, and third Tuesday of September.

GREENWOOD COUNTY.—First Tuesday of January, April and September.

BUTLER COUNTY.—First Tuesday of March and second Tuesday of June and November.

FOURTEENTH DISTRICT.

THOMAS J. FLANNELLY, Judge; residence, Independence.

MONTGOMERY COUNTY.—First Monday of February, May and October.

FIFTEENTH DISTRICT.

RICHARD M. PICKLER, Judge; residence, Smith Center.

MITCHELL COUNTY.—Second Monday of January, third Monday of April, and fourth Monday of September.

OSBORNE COUNTY.—First Monday of February, second Monday of May, and third Monday of October.

JEWELL COUNTY.—First Monday of March and June and second Monday of November.

SMITH COUNTY.—Fourth Monday of March, first Monday of September, and first Monday of December.

SIXTEENTH DISTRICT.

ELMER C. CLARK, Judge; residence, Parsons.

LABETTE COUNTY.—At Oswego, first Tuesday of February, May and October; at Parsons, first Tuesday of March, June and November.

SEVENTEENTH DISTRICT.

W. S. LANGMADE, Judge; residence, Oberlin.

PHILLIPS COUNTY.—Second Monday of January, third Monday of April, and first Monday of September.

NORTON COUNTY.—First Monday of February and May and third Monday of September.

DECATUR COUNTY.—Fourth Monday of February and second Monday of May and October.

RAWLINS COUNTY.—Third Monday of March and May and second Monday of November.

CHEYENNE COUNTY.—First Monday of April and December and fourth Monday of May.

EIGHTEENTH DISTRICT.

THOMAS C. WILSON, Judge, first division; residence, Wichita.

THORNTON W. SARGENT, Judge, second division; residence, Wichita.

SEDGWICK COUNTY.—Second Monday of January, First Monday of April, and first Monday of October.

NINETEENTH DISTRICT.

CARROLL L. SWARTS, Judge; residence, Winfield.

SUMNER COUNTY.—First Tuesday of January, May and September.

COWLEY COUNTY.—First Tuesday of March, June and November.

TWENTIETH DISTRICT.

D. A. BANTA, Judge; residence, Great Bend.

RICE COUNTY.—First Tuesday of January, April and September.

BARTON COUNTY.—First Tuesday of March and June and third Tuesday of November.

STAFFORD COUNTY.—First Tuesday of February, May and October.

TWENTY-FIRST DISTRICT.

SAM KIMBLE, Judge; residence, Manhattan.

RILEY COUNTY.—First Monday of January and third Monday of April and September.

MARSHALL COUNTY.—First Monday of February, May and October.

CLAY COUNTY.—First Monday of March, June and November.

TWENTY-SECOND DISTRICT.

WILLIAM I. STUART, Judge; residence, Troy.

DONIPHAN COUNTY.—First Monday of January, April and October.

BROWN COUNTY.—First Monday of February, May and November.

NEMAHA COUNTY.—First Monday of March, September and December.

TWENTY-THIRD DISTRICT.

J. C. RUPPENTHAL, Judge; residence, Russell.

RUSSELL COUNTY.—First Monday of January, May and September.

ELLIS COUNTY.—First Tuesday of February, June and October.

TREGO COUNTY.—Third Tuesday of March and September.

GOVE COUNTY.—Third Tuesday of April and October.

LOGAN COUNTY.—Fourth Tuesday of April and October.

WALLACE COUNTY.—Third Tuesday of May and November.

TWENTY-FOURTH DISTRICT.

PRESTON B. GILLETT, Judge; residence, Kingman.

KINGMAN COUNTY.—Third Monday of March, fourth Monday of June and first Monday of December.

PRATT COUNTY.—First Monday of March, second Monday of June and second Monday of November.

BARBER COUNTY.—Second Monday of February, second Monday of May and second Monday of October.

HARPER COUNTY.—Second Monday of January, third Monday of April and second Monday of September.

TWENTY-NINTH DISTRICT.

EDWARD L. FISHER, Judge, first division; residence, Kansas City.

F. D. HUTCHINGS, Judge, second division; residence, Kansas City.

H. J. SMITH, Judge, third division; residence, Kansas City.

WYANDOTTE COUNTY.—First Monday of March and June, second Monday of September and first Monday of December.

THIRTIETH DISTRICT.

DALLAS GROVER, Judge; residence, Ellsworth.

OTTAWA COUNTY.—First Tuesday of January and April and third Tuesday of September.

SALINE COUNTY.—Second Tuesday of March and fourth Tuesday of August and November.

ELLSWORTH COUNTY.—Fourth Tuesday of January and April and second Tuesday of October.

LINCOLN COUNTY.—Third Tuesday of February and May and second Tuesday of November.

THIRTY-FIRST DISTRICT.

GORDON L. FINLEY, Judge; residence, Dodge City.

FORD COUNTY.—Third Tuesday of January and second Tuesday of June and September.

KIOWA COUNTY.—First Tuesday of May and second Tuesday of October.

CLARK COUNTY.—Third Tuesday of February and fourth Tuesday of September.

MEADE COUNTY.—Third Tuesday of March and fourth Tuesday of October.

GRAY COUNTY.—Second Tuesday of April and November.

COMANCHE COUNTY.—Third Tuesday of May and first Tuesday of December.

THIRTY-SECOND DISTRICT.

GEORGE J. DOWNER, Judge; residence, Syracuse.

FINNEY COUNTY.—Second Monday of January, May and September.

HAMILTON COUNTY.—Second Monday of February, fourth Monday of May and second Monday of November.

KEARNY COUNTY.—First Monday of February and May and third Monday of November.

HASKELL COUNTY.—First Monday of April and fourth Monday of September.

STEVENS COUNTY.—Thursday following the first Monday of April and Thursday following the fourth Monday of September and second Monday in December.

STANTON COUNTY.—Third Monday of April and second Monday of October.

MORTON COUNTY.—Wednesday following the third Monday of April and Wednesday following the second Monday of October.

GRANT COUNTY.—Friday following the third Monday of April and Friday following the second Monday of October.

SEWARD COUNTY.—Fourth Monday of February, first Monday of June and first Monday of December.

THIRTY-THIRD DISTRICT.

A. S. FOULKS, Judge; residence, Ness City.

RUSH COUNTY.—First Monday of February, second Monday of May and third Monday of September.

NESS COUNTY.—Second Monday of February, fourth Monday of April and fourth Monday of September.

LANE COUNTY.—Third Monday of February, first Monday of May and Wednesday following the fourth Monday of September.

SCOTT COUNTY.—Fourth Monday of February, third Monday of May and first Monday of October.

WICHITA COUNTY.—Fourth Tuesday of January, third Tuesday of April and Wednesday following the first Monday of October.

THIRTY-THIRD DISTRICT—*concluded.*

GREELEY COUNTY.—Third Tuesday of January, second Tuesday of April and Thursday following the first Monday of October.

PAWNEE COUNTY.—First Monday of March, fourth Monday of May and first Monday of November.

EDWARDS COUNTY.—Third Monday of March, first Monday of June and third Monday of November.

HODGEMAN COUNTY.—First Monday of April, second Monday of June and first Monday of December.

THIRTY-FOURTH DISTRICT.

CHARLES W. SMITH, Judge; residence, Stockton.

ROOKS COUNTY.—Second Tuesday of January and first Tuesday of May and September.

GRAHAM COUNTY.—First Tuesday of February and third Tuesday of May and September.

SHERIDAN COUNTY.—Fourth Tuesday of February and first Tuesday of June and October.

THOMAS COUNTY.—Third Tuesday of March and June and first Tuesday of November.

SHERMAN COUNTY.—First Tuesday of April and July and third Tuesday of November.

THIRTY-FIFTH DISTRICT.

ROBERT C. HEIZER, Judge; residence, Osage City.

POTTAWATOMIE COUNTY.—First Tuesday of April and September and second Tuesday of December.

WABAUNSEE COUNTY.—First Tuesday of February, May and October.

OSAGE COUNTY.—Second Tuesday of March, June and November.

THIRTY-SIXTH DISTRICT.

OSCAR RAINES, Judge; residence, Oskaloosa.

JACKSON COUNTY.—Second Monday of January, first Monday of May and third Monday of September.

JEFFERSON COUNTY.—First Monday of March, first Monday of June and first Monday of November.

THIRTY-SEVENTH DISTRICT.

OSCAR FOUST, Judge; residence, Iola.

ALLEN COUNTY.—Second Tuesday of January, May and September.

WOODSON COUNTY.—Second Tuesday of March and June and the Tuesday succeeding the second Monday of November.

THIRTY-EIGHTH DISTRICT.

A. J. CURRAN, Judge; residence, Pittsburg.

CRAWFORD COUNTY.—At Girard, second Monday of January, first Monday of April and first Monday of October; at Pittsburg, third Monday of February, second Monday of May and third Monday of November.

CPSIA information can be obtained
at www.ICGtesting.com
Printed in the USA
BVHW041408151121
621700BV00008B/263